MW00639999

Venus
and
Adonis

The Magic of Love

by Owen S. Rachleff

designed by Roland Rodegast

The C. R. Gibson Company, Norwalk, Connecticut

Printed in the United States of America
Library of Congress Catalog Card Number: 73-88089
ISBN: 0-8378-1752-8

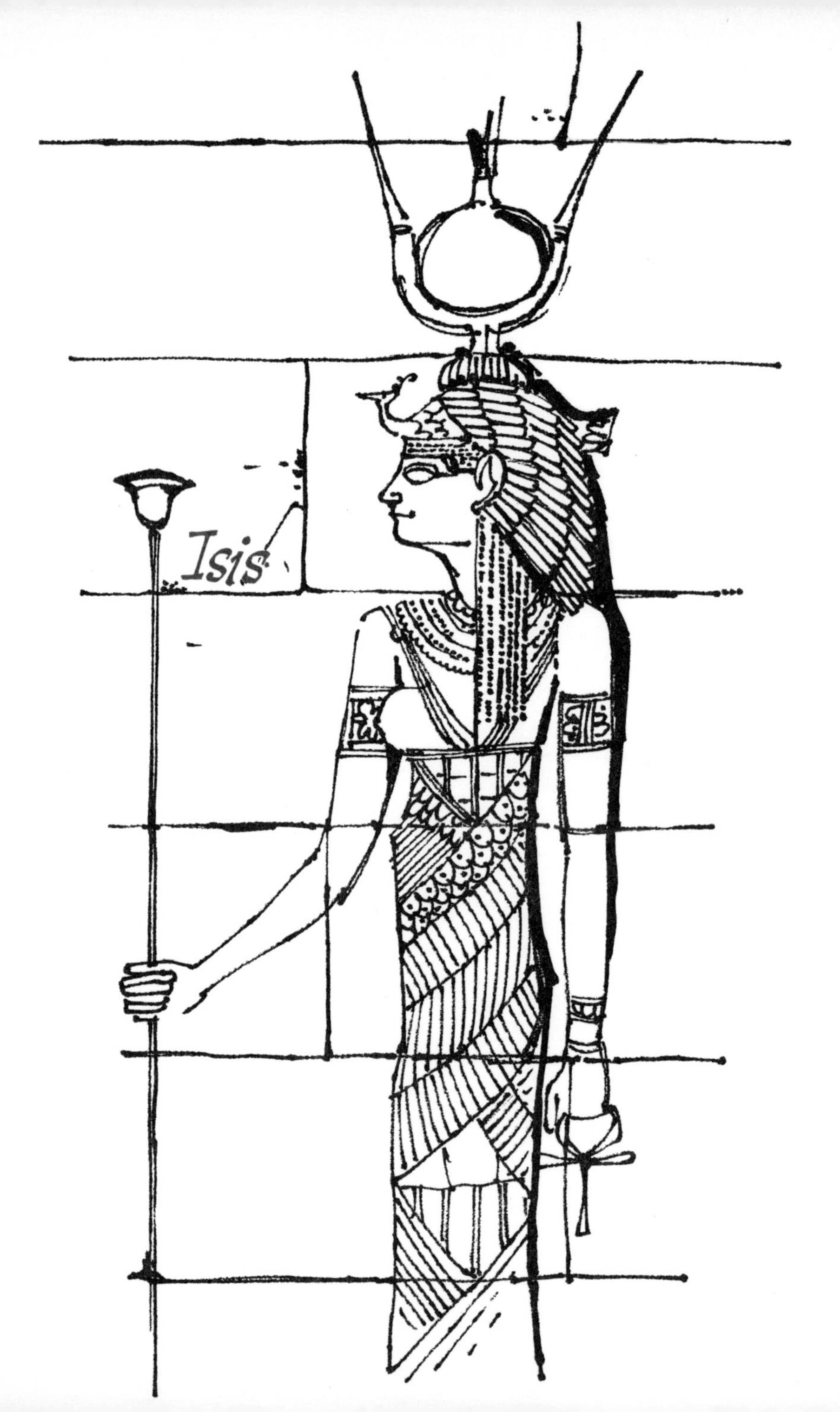
Isis

Introduction

"Love, your magic spell is everywhere . . ." so goes the popular song. In the ancient world, this was a prevailing thought. Love and magic went hand in hand, for if magic was a system of unexplained wonderment, what wonderment could be more mysterious than that of love, love which conquers all, love which — according to an old Scottish poet — ". . . is like a dizziness; it winna let a poor body gang about his business."

To understand this "dizziness" all the better, the ancient sorcerers and magicians sought to find items or gestures in everyday life that could explain, enhance and insure love, that omnipresent emotion which seemed to be as furtive as it was forceful.

The first glimmerings of what might be called love magic go back before the dawn of civilization to the crude heavy-set votive figures of "Mother Earth" — the prototype love goddess — found in prehistoric graves and archeological digs of southern Europe. These simple clay figures — symbols of fertility and sex — were later refined into the goddesses of the early religions. As such they were not merely fertility figures, but rather idealized versions of Love itself. Since a goddess, of course, was mistress of magic and miracles these early love goddesses were therefore commonly invoked to magically insure a happy love life or ease the pain of unrequited love.

Modern supplicants in the realm of love might like to know who these Eastern Love Queens were lest today they feel inclined to offer an appropriate prayer or invocation.

Perhaps the earliest deity associated entirely with "amour" was Lilith, the legendary figure who is supposed to have been Adam's first wife in Eden. According to Hebrew folklore, Lilith was created with Adam; he by God, she by Satan. Because of her tempestuous and Satanic nature, Lilith would not obey her husband or allow herself to be relegated to domestic tasks. As a result of this, the couple quarreled and Lilith fled Eden, whereupon she became a sort of love demon, especially invoked by witches in the Middle Ages who believed she was responsible for tormentingly erotic dreams. In short, Lilith was the succubus, or female sex spirit, of demonology.

A far more refined and gentle love goddess was Isis of ancient Egypt. Wife of the beneficent Osiris — god of agriculture and peace — Isis ruled marriage, medicinal magic and domestic affairs. She was thus worshiped particularly by women who represented her seated with the feather of Truth in her hair and the Ankh, or life cross, in her hand.

Isis learned the secrets of love and the universe from the sun god Ra, who relied upon her for magical cures in his old age. In the same way, those smitten by love call upon "Heavenly Isis . . . to bestow thy soothing medicine."

In Mesopotamia the love goddess was the volatile Ishtar (sometimes Astar or Astarte). She was capricious in love and pitiless in vengeance against men and gods who spurned her advances. Thus she became a figure of veneration for downtrodden women who regarded her as a liberated life force.

Ishtar loved the handsome Tammuz for a while, but when bored, consigned him to the nether regions. Afterwards, lonely and remorseful, Ishtar resurrected her dead lover and thus became a Spring goddess as well as a mistress of love.

In Babylon, Ishtar was represented as a dark-haired, star-studded queen, adorned in much jewelry and sprinkling waters of passion on the world. Her devotees often called upon Ishtar to shed these precious drops on them so that they, like her, might be endowed with allurement.

To these goddesses and others, and especially to Venus (see page 24) did the legendary Dr. Faust turn his prayers when he sought youth and love. Hearing this, Mephistopheles, the devil's emissary, appeared and promised Faust all his heart could desire as well as the love of ancient deities and queens.

The great German poet Goethe, in his play *Faust,* sets forth the promise of sorcery as in fact a promise of love. Mephistopheles puts it this way to the world-weary Faust:

"My friend," he says, "you'll get more from my magic to delight your senses than ever you could get from a year of dull scholarship. All that the lovely spirits sing, all their pretty pictures, I will bring. Not mere idle sorcery, they will tickle your fancies and steep your soul in pleasure and passion. . ."

What Mephistopheles doesn't say is that in payment for these delights Faust will be forever damned, "ruined in the end." But till such time, the spirits of love await him, and he must venerate their sorcery.

Invocation of the love gods and reverence for their powers is not always enough. Ancient people — and many moderns — resort to specific formulas and incantations in order to achieve their hearts' desire with the aid of magic.

The Egyptians, the Greeks, the Romans, the Hindus and the sorcerers of Africa were especially productive when it came to these nostrums. As Mr. John Wellington Wells said of the Sorcerer of Gilbert and Sullivan, they seem to have been dealers in "magic and spells, in blessings and curses and ever-filled purses, in prophesies, witches and knells."

The Egyptian Love Knot

The Egyptians of the time of the pharaohs were a practical folk. Besides imploring Isis and the cat goddess Bast to aid them in amorous adventures, they also concocted a clever love knot — a bit complicated in execution but avowed to be romantically effective.

According to an ancient magical papyrus, one must take a piece of fine linen — about fifteen inches long — striped green, blue, red and white and lay it out flat. The linen is then stained with a few drops of blood secured from the hoopoe bird, whose tail is also striped. Apparently the stripes of the cloth and of the bird will act as symbolic bonds to the one you love.

After the linen band is stained, one must catch a scarab, or sacred beetle, dedicated to the Sun God Ra, drown it quickly and wrap it in byssus (a form of ancient silk). The wrapped scarab is now placed in the center of the linen band, which is next folded over to cover the little package. Now it is necessary to bind and tie this cloth around the body — or head — of the loved one. As a subterfuge one might suggest that the band is useful as a cold compress for headache — or as a decorative headdress in the Eastern style.

Once the stripped band with beetle is properly in place, the "victim" will fall hopelessly in love with the one who prepared the knot. A result well worth the sacrifice of hoopoe and beetle.

The Greek Love Spell of Simaetha

Simaetha was a Greek maiden smitten by love for Delphis, a handsome shepherd who was, alas, indifferent to her. The poet Theocritus — born about 310 B.C. in Syracuse — immortalized the lovers in an idyl and included therein a love spell which Simaetha was obliged to prepare.

For twelve days Delphis ignored her, "nor once has he knocked at my door," she lamented "nor knows whether I am alive or dead . . .

unkind that he is! Tomorrow I shall go to the wrestling school to see my love and to reproach him with the wrong he is doing me. But for now I will bewitch him with my enchantments."

Calling upon the moon goddess, Selene, the love goddess, Aphrodite, and the goddess of magic and witchcraft, Hecate, Simaetha prepared the following spell:

Into a flame three laurel leaves are dropped one by one; thus will the lover's arrogance be diminished. As this is done the supplicant utters the following prayer: "Magic wheel, draw home to me the one I love."

Next wax is melted in the flame so that the lover's heart will melt with love; the prayer is repeated.

Then husks of barley are now burned to break down the lover's resistance — his (or her) hard shell; the prayer is uttered again.

While the flame still burns, the supplicant takes a thread from a garment of the beloved and tosses it also into the flame, thus to send the fire of passion to his heart; "Magic wheel, draw home to me the one I love," this is said even as the thread is burned.

Now it is required that water be slowly poured over the flame in honor of Selene, the moon goddess and mistress of the tides. Thus will the loved one be cleansed of all thoughts that may inhibit love. At the same time the lovelorn must invoke the moon goddess as follows:

"Think upon my love and whence it came, O Selene."

Finally, the supplicant gathers up a paste of ashes — the result of pouring libations over the flame — and places this residue of laurel, wax, and barley husks in a bowl entwined with bright red wool. Turning the bowl clockwise, the final entreaty is made: "Magic wheel, draw home to me the one I love."

Hopefully, as Delphis came to Simaetha's bed, so will your love respond to you.

Love Spells from India

The Indians worshiped Rama Krishna, the beautiful love god, and exalted the pleasures of love in sculpture and in poetry. A lovely veda, or epic in Sanskrit, offers incantations for securing the love of a man, on the one hand, and of a woman on the other.

To secure a man's love: Five small red candles are ignited (for the five solar deities) along with incense of sandalwood, strawberry or cinnamon, all pleasing to Rama Krishna. Vanilla bean may also be burned, for its elegant aroma — an aroma of love — was conceived by Rama Krishna.

The supplicant invokes the Hindu gods Maruts, of storms; Agni, the fire god and Apsaras the seductive love nymph, to wit:

"I am possessed by burning love for this man, O Agni, fire god (for whom the red flame burns). This love comes to me from Apsaras inspired by Krishna (for whom the fragrances smolder). Let this man yearn for me, desire me, let his desire burn for me! Let his love come forth from the air (aided by Maruts), enter him (even as the fragrance permeates the room).

"Let him desire me as nothing has been desired before. I love him, want him, he must feel the same desire for me! O Maruts, let him become filled with love. O Agni, let him burn with love for me!"

The candles should burn down at this point. One must then sleep in the fragrant air thinking on Rama Krishna and the love act if the spell is to work. By the dawn the love smitten man will appear, ardent, aroused, seeking his sweetheart. He will drop at her feet, kiss her fingers, her toes — he will not stop . . .

To secure a woman's love: Burn five small white candles (for the five solar gods) along with the fragrance of musk (a favorite scent of the love goddess, Lakshmi). An arrow is taken — it may be a rod affixed with feathers and a point — and held over the candle fires while the following is invoked:

"With this all powerful arrow of love do I pierce thy heart, O woman! Love, love that causes unease that will overcome thee, let love fly on this arrow straight and true to your heart. It has the point of my love, its shaft is my determination to possess thee."

The arrow is then plunged into one of the flames.

"Yea, thy heart is pierced," says the lovelorn. "The arrow has struck home. I have overcome thee by these acts! Come to me, submissive, without pride. Even thy mother will be powerless to prevent thy coming, neither shall thy father be able to prevent thee! Thou art completely in my power."

The flaming tip of the arrow is then plunged in water and the resultant smoke inhaled while the name of Varuna — the all-seeing god — is invoked. The lover then closes his eyes and tries to sleep amid the musky fragrance, while the candles burn themselves out. By the morrow the woman, lovesick and trembling, weak of will, submissive, her hair disordered, her lips quivering for kisses will appear at the lover's door and fall forcefully into his ardent arms.

The Love Cakes of Rome

The Roman poet Tibullus (1st century B.C.) writes of the cakes by which the vestal virgins — Roman priestesses who were keepers of the sacred fire — secured love for those who revered them. Both the recipe and the invocation have come down to us.

Three small cakes are made of flour, leavening, water and salt. The compound is then squeezed into a phallic shape and rolled in poppy seeds, which are symbols of female fertility. The cakes are then baked until risen.

With cakes resting on a round cloth the supplicant recites:

"This cake by me made, let it contain all powers of love such as Hecate — the witch goddess — possesses. Thrice will I sprinkle each with salt [which you must do]. Thus nine times have I sprinkled [nine is the ultimate digit and a magic number] and I devote these cakes to Hecate, even as did Medea before me."

Now you must eat one cake, feed another to the one you love — but do not tell him it is a love cake lest you offend the goddess — and the third is for Hecate herself, who will receive it if you bury it, in a nine-inch hole, beneath the moon, "in silent night . . ." as Tibullus tells us.

The Yam Ritual of Africa

From Black Africa comes the story of Onyame, god of sunshine, who sought to inspire men and women with the secrets of love. Onyame called upon Legba, the earth god of masculinity (symbolized by his club) and of femininity (symbolized by his breasts) to institute love making among mortals. But unfortunately, neither god could communicate with men. So they devised a plan. Into the earth they planted the delicious yam; and when a certain woman discovered it — admiring its impressive shape — they caused her to wonder how she might prepare it for the man she loved. They made her take the yam to him whereupon Legba inspired her to place the yam in a mortar, while Onyame caused her to pick up the pestle. At last the woman realized what to do and began pounding the yam, thrusting the pestle up and down into the mortar.

By this act, the man and the woman realized the secrets of love and thus did Legba and Onyame achieve their will.

Some say an effective love ritual is to repeat that ancient pounding while chanting the names of Legba and Onyame. Descendants of the ancient Africans may be especially effective in this performance.

What to do: Take a soft yam, place it peeled in a bowl (or mortar) with a little water or wine, and with a pestle slowly mash it, up and down, up and down, murmuring: Legba; Legba (twice, because this god is both male and female); Onyame (pronounced O-nee-á-mee). When the yam is fully reduced, place one finger into it and repeat your loved one's name three times (three is a number of generation).

In some cases supplicants may wish to blend the yam pulp into a cake or other edible and feed it to the object of your desire. Or you may eat some yourself, always thinking of love and the loved one as those in love are wont to do.

2 Divinations of Love

According to the gypsies — who are alleged to be gifted seers — there are several means of divining or fortelling various aspects of one's love life and fortune concerning affairs of the heart. These areas of love magic will now be explored.

The Love Secrets of the Palm

Your own hand, specifically your palm, may reveal much in terms of fortune and love if you are well versed in the gypsy methods of cheiromancy — palm reading — and especially if you know which line refers to what.

Taking the left palm as our guide, since this is the palm closest to the heart, we look for the love line, or heart line, which is essential in readings regarding "amour." This line usually runs across the topmost part of the palm just beneath the soft mounds at the base of each finger. In some cases this heart line extends the whole way from the index finger to the small finger. Sometimes it is deep and well-etched. In such cases we are dealing with an ardent subject, one for whom love and affairs of the heart are wide in scope and deep in meaning. This will be especially true if the line of fate — which runs upwards from the wrist — cuts through the heart line. A life of love is to be the fate of those who bear such palms.

But will it be sweet love or will there be heartaches and recriminations? For this, say the gypsies, we must look to the mounds, the fleshy bumps usually apparent on the palm. Two are definitely connected with love magic. The large Mound of Venus, which forms the ball under the thumb, and the Mound of Jupiter, which is the ball beneath the index finger. A well-developed Mound of Venus, etched with many fine lines, indicates a sensitive, amorous individual likely to experience many affairs of the heart. This is especially true if the heart line is long and deep.

When the heart line rises into the Mound of Jupiter, one can be sure that love affairs will be successful in the main and that you yourself may be counted on as a reliable, faithful partner. Should your heart line stop short of the Jupiter Mound, however, the indications are that yours will be an up-and-down love life; one that often stops short of a full and rich relationship.

Such dire indications, however, may be mitigated by a well-developed Mound of Venus, especially if the heart line runs close to the head line (the line parallel to the heart line towards the center of the palm). This denotes an emotional life well governed by the intellect and therefore probably fulfilling.

There are further ramifications of these essential lines and mounds, according to lore. Weakly etched heart lines, in conjunction with strong destiny lines, and well-developed mounds, indicate a calm but happy love life. A small Mound of Venus with few lines criss-crossing it denotes reserve, perhaps timidity — or refined, gentle feelings easily hurt.

Those with delicate lines throughout, small mounds and tight skin are likely to be a bit "uptight" themselves in terms of love and passion. They must be treated with kid gloves, so to speak. Happily, lines will often develop and deepen (especially on the right palm) as one lives his life and enjoys the various experiences it has to offer.

In studying the palm of your beloved look for depth of lines and height of mounds. If they are consistent, yours will be a passionate (sometimes hectic) relationship. If moderate or incomplete, look for

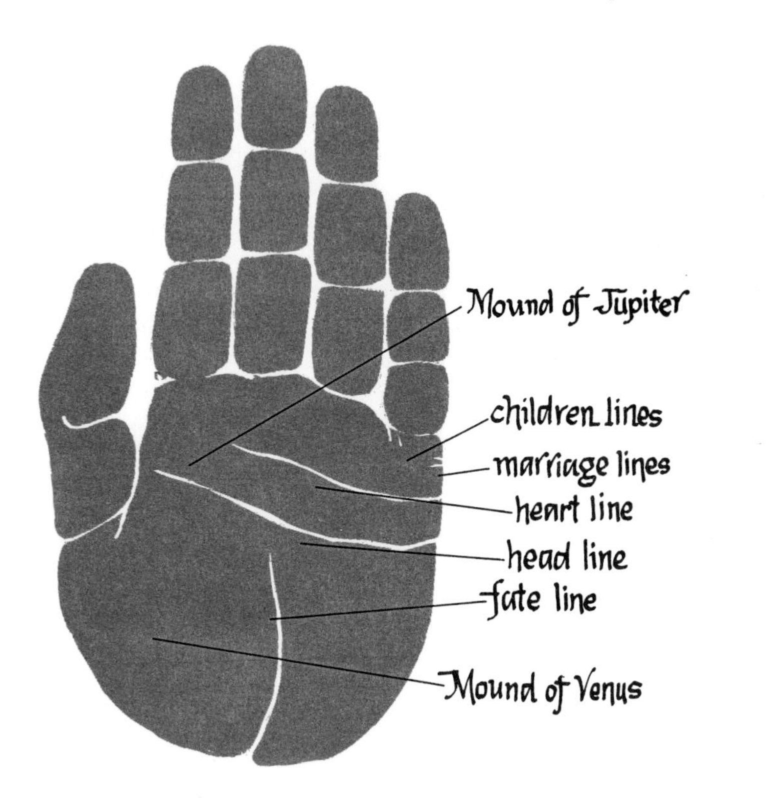

sensitive, sometimes hesitating attitudes to love (gentle coaxing will help such persons). Weak lines and mounds can mean passivity, reluctance, even rejection. Proceed with caution here, say the seers, lest you be disappointed.

Marriage and Children

The old gypsies can foretell — so they say — marriage and the number of children one will have by the tiny creases near the little finger. The number of lines at that spot, however, does not always correspond to the exact number of marriages or of children, but rather to opportunities and qualities of same.

The marriage lines are horizontal, near the edge of the hand, below the "pinky." Marriage lines close to the heart line indicate an early wedding — between the ages of 18 and 22. Lines farther up show marriage between 25 and 35, and horizontal lines crowding the pinky mean a late marriage — if at all.

Sloping marriage lines may mean life as a bachelor, or spinster. The down variety will be reserved; the ones that swing upward will also likely "swing."

Very deep marriage lines may mean more than one connubial bond or one that is very long and successful, especially if the heart line and Mound of Venus are notable.

Children lines, the gypsies say, are more apparent on female hands than on male and on the left hand particularly. They are the vertical strokes above the marriage line. Usually they indicate the number of children — one line per child. But in some cases, if they are very numerous and very deep, the indication is of one happy child who dominates the marriage.

Single persons with children lines need not be alarmed or ashamed. These represent possibilities, whether realized or not. In some cases, say the seers, your "children" may be close friends, relatives — or even pets.

The Cards

Perhaps the best known gypsy of them all is Carmen, the protagonist of the famous French opera. In the third act, Carmen spreads her shawl before the campfire and begins to lay out a deck of playing cards in order to tell her fortune. Two friends do the same. They are lucky in their venture — Carmen is not. Where they read of love and wealth and success, Carmen consistently turns up the ace of spades: "A grave," as she says.

How does Carmen — or any gypsy — know what the cards purport? This is their venerable technique:

Spades are traditionally symbolic of death, trouble or despair.

One spade alone — the ace — usually means a grave, two spades: a lover's quarrel, the King and Queen of spades indicate menacing figures of authority and the Jack is a troublemaker.

Similar readings may be made for clubs, which are signs of business associates, social intercourse and stress. An ace of clubs means speculation, the King and Queen of clubs refer to business associates and the Jack is described by one authority as "a dark young man very much in love."

This brings us to the red suits — or the lucky cards — the ones of love and fortune. Hearts quite naturally are signs of love and matters of affection, such as family affairs. Diamonds give us portents of wealth or travel.

Specifically, an ace of hearts is the sign of singular devotion, the King and Queen of hearts are figures of fidelity and love — your parents perhaps — the Jack is a lover. In diamonds, the ace may mean a letter relating good news; the King and Queen refer to visitors or bearers of glad tidings and the Jack is, according to one tradition, a postman or soldier.

We have not revealed the significance of every card, but one can surmise the meanings of the number cards by knowing the rules of numerology, which connotes each digit as follows: Number 1 signifies leadership, purpose, unity; Number 2 is divisive, two-faced, sensitive; 3 denotes generation, wisdom, business acumen; 4 is a morose number, but also signifies reliability and thrift; 5 is a bright fortunate number, a sign of intellect; 6 may be called the emotional or amorous number (the six of hearts is a strong card of love potential) and of artistic quality; 7 represents the mystic, the innovative and noble soul, while 8 is the number of contrast, great failure or great success — perhaps recklessness. Finally, Number 9 stands for high mindedness, religious feeling and noble sacrifice. (10 is simply 1 all over again: $1 + 0 = 1$)

In laying out the cards it is naturally of great importance to study which card lies next to which. For the interreaction of the symbols is the truest key to fortune — so say the gypsies.

To begin, one takes the date and adds up the factors as follows: February 21, 1975 — February is the second month (2), 21st day is a three because 2 plus 1 equals 3; 1975 ($1 + 9 + 7 + 5$) equals 22 or 4, because $2 + 2 = 4$. The total of these numbers is 9. Thus nine cards are to be used. (If the date totals less than four add seven more cards.)

With a nine-card layout taken from a well-shuffled deck, the gypsies can learn much. Spread out the deck face down, and select nine cards which are placed in a row face down. Turn up the center card first. This indicates you, the reader. Since we are dealing with love magic let us say that the first card is the six of hearts, a strong love card as already indicated. A Jack of spades to the left of this card and an eight of diamonds to its right could mean that you (the center card) will be inclined to direct your amorous attention to an attractive rascal (the Jack) who is probably after your money (indicated by the eight of diamonds). The affair may be a disaster or a whirlwind of romance: remember eight is a number of contrast.

A happier reading of nine cards is now shown: left to right — Ace of diamonds, five of clubs, Queen of diamonds, seven of clubs, six of hearts (you), Jack of hearts, seven of spades, King of hearts, three of clubs. One may make the following interpretation. You (the center card, or six of hearts) a person seeking love, will receive a letter (ace of diamonds) indicating a lady visitor (Queen of diamonds) who probably bears good news or financial gifts (five of clubs), as well as a meaningful message (seven of clubs). This message may pertain to the charming young man (Jack of hearts) who is as yet unsettled in his attitude toward you (seven of spades). An older, loving figure (King of hearts), perhaps your father, will most likely bolster your romance with encouragement and wisdom (three of clubs).

There are many interpretations possible for the same layout. A man reading the above, for example, may substitute himself for the Jack or King and see in the six of hearts the object of his heart's desire. A certain amount of sensibility and logic will always aid even the most "inspired" reading.

The Tarot Cards of Love

More specific, and some say more rewarding, are the ancient tarot cards which have come down from far-off Arabia and which, according to some seers, represent mystic symbols of love, fortune and fate.

The tarot cards are generally divided into two groups: the minor arcana (56 cards) which correspond to the hearts, clubs, spades and diamonds of the playing deck. In this case Wands (clubs) equal business; Cups (hearts) love; Swords (spades) strife and Pentacles (diamonds) money or wealth.

The more revealing group of tarot cards are those of the major arcana (22 cards) which are the famous picture cards heavy with symbolism, numerology and elements of the mystic Cabala. To read these cards apparently takes great skill, insight and knowledge. Various schools, of course, give various interpretations and various layouts. The pyramid layout, for example, is used by some, as is the date layout, described above. The popular Celtic Cross is favored by others. In this, six cards are arranged like a cross with two at the center, one overturned (signifying the person to be divined) and one face down on top of him (a destiny card).

Whether a card is head up or foot up (reversed) is essential.

Generally speaking well-aspected (right-side up) cards are positive and ill-aspected cards indicate negative readings.

The tarot cards of love are generally these: the High Priestess (reversed) equals sensual pleasure; the Empress (up) marriage; the Emperor (up) marriage for a man; the Lovers (up) attraction, beauty, love — but if reversed: wrong choice in relationship; the Charioteer (reversed) decadent desires; Strength, or the Lion Tamer, (up) triumph of love; the Star (up) spiritual love; the Moon (up) fantasy-ridden love affairs; the Sun (up) happy family life and marriage.

To elucidate the above: if in a layout, the High Priestess (reversed) is to the left of the Lovers (up), the Sun (up) and the Charioteer (reversed), the seers might say that purely sensuous or carnal desires (the Priestess and the Charioteer) may tend to overwhelm a meaningful relationship (the Lovers) and dominate marriage (the Sun).

If Strength is the player card, then we see that good sense will probably triumph and love will be rich, meaningful and fulfilling.

Of course, if the player card should be the well-known Hanged Man — a symbol of indecision and suspense — then one must guard against confusion and, above all, temptation — often the by-products of amour.

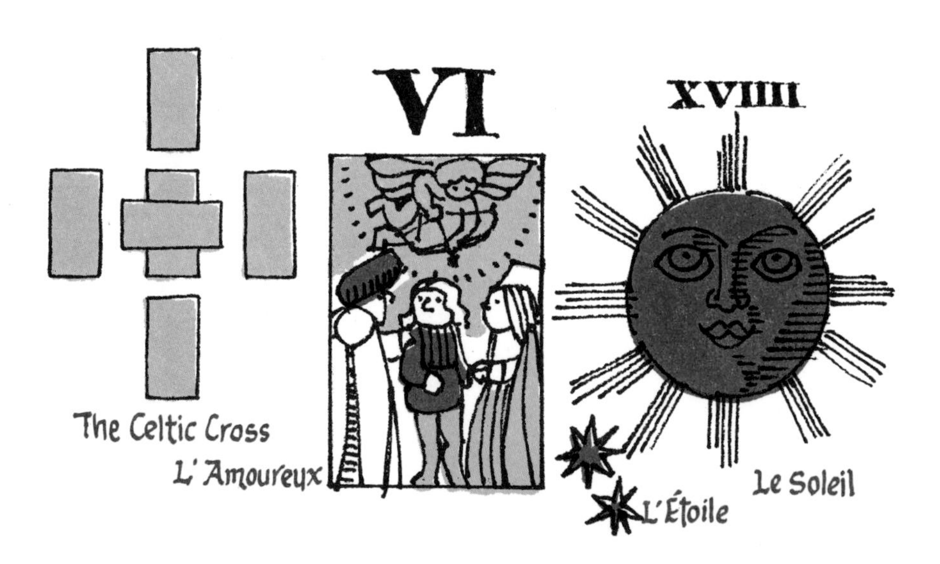

Venus, The Love Goddess Par Excellence

The strongest love factor in astrology, and indeed in many other forms of divination, is the figure — or planet — of Venus, long since crowned Queen of love, beauty, sensuous desire and sex.

To Shakespeare, Venus is the ardent pursuer of the reluctant Adonis, before whom "stands she in trembling ecstasy . . .". The medieval minstrel Tannhäuser hails her as the goddess of love and song. "Thou art the source of all in life we treasure . . .", he sings.

The old astrologers regarded Venus in the heavens as the chief influence regarding love and art, the ruler of Friday, the "star of Eve," of gentleness, charm, seductiveness, a love of jewelry, flowers and perfumes. Those she rules — or in whose horoscopes she appears — are usually full-lipped, soft in body and sensuous in movement.

Venus adores contrast. She will be at ease with the artist or with the courtesan; she favors a delicate scent like cinnamon or a flaming red silk scarf.

In the sign of Taurus she imparts tender feelings to those who are consumed by desire. To Scorpios she excites delightful passions; in Cancer she means romantic poetry; the Gemini twins are blessed with fidelity by Venus; Leo's pride is enhanced, especially towards family; Virgo gains nobility, feminine grace, while Libra seeks balance in love affairs. Sagittarius, the archer, aims for his loved one's heart when Venus is nigh and Capricorn is playful, even erotic in her presence. Aries, the ram of the Golden Fleece, dreams of adventurous love when Venus is in his sphere and the beneficent Aquarius bestows grace and charm to those around him. The fish called Pisces are especially proud, since legend tells us that one of them was actually Venus herself in disguise; the other, Cupid, her son. One must make sure in the above readings to know his *correct* Zodiac designation and not be misled by the outdated system. (See the author's "Sky Diamonds: the New Astrology")

The Mound of Venus has earlier been discussed in palmistry; it is the zone of love. Here especially dwells Cupid, the child of Venus, who — with his magic arrows dipped in fire — ignites erotic as well as amorous emotions.

The goddess is, of course, patroness of several lucky charms, stones and colors sacred to love and, according to the ancient Romans who worshiped her, useful in conquests of the heart. Here is a table called the *Treasury of Venus* to enumerate these magical attributes.

Plants and flowers associated with Venus: myrtle, almond trees, honeysuckle, mistletoe, iris, forget-me-not, daisy, rose

Animals: turtle doves, nightingale, pigeon, sheep, sparrow, butterflies

Colors: pink and green

Metal: Copper

Gems: Emerald, coral

Scents: Musk, rose, aloewood

Her symbol is the mirror: ♀

Her secret names: Aphrodite, Cytherea, Ishtar, Venere.

She is the source of all things venerable, Venusian and of concepts which are venereal.

Her influence in love magic is best summed up by the poet Homer as he describes her first appearance before the gods: "Wonder seized them all," he writes, "as they saw the violet-crowned Cytherea."

The Moon

Close behind Venus in amorous influence is Selene, the moon goddess. Indeed the role of the moon in love is almost proverbial, a factor examined in mysticism, in poetry and even in psychology, where allegedly moon-struck persons are called lunatics (from Luna or moon), and are said to be governed by fantasy, imagination and unbridled desire — the ancient attributes of Selene.

In astrology the moon symbolizes fantasy and romance, sometimes romantic sorrow, as in the case of unrequited love. Shakespeare's Juliet fears such an influence when she warns Romeo: "O! swear not by the moon, the inconstant moon, that monthly changes in her circled orb, lest that thy love prove likewise variable."

The magnetic force of the moon, greatly valued by mystics, is said to "turn its devotees into fantastic and changeable beings . . . listless, apathetic, undecided . . .": in short "moony" types.

Indeed, when the moon is in conjunction with Venus, in the horoscope, according to the old astrology, one may expect a love-dominated life. Lovesickness will result. On the other hand, great romance may be the lot of moon-governed Venusians, like Cleopatra or Helen of Troy.

It is said that the moon dominates the Zodiac sign of Cancer, whose natives are thus known as Moon Children. All lovers may look to the moon for signals of destiny and romance, as witness this venerable Moon Oracle offered to maidens seeking love.

"Young ladies," it begins, "starting with the first day of May on which the full moon is visible, look at it on seven consecutive evenings, having a small mirror hidden in your pocket or your hand. Then on the night of the seventh day place this mirror under your pillow, begging that Selene show you in a dream your future husband or lover. On the morrow, go out early and give alms to the first beggar you meet. If it is a man, you will be married within a year to the man of whom you dreamt [not to the beggar!] If it is a woman that you meet, you will have to wait another year."

Males who seek their fortune by the moon should invoke Endymion, the handsome youth taken to the moon by the goddess Diana and left there to sleep away eternity. His face is visible on the full moon to this day, eyes closed, lips pursed for kissing. If you see Endymion over your right shoulder, unexpectedly, say the seers, love will be yours that very night — a love of surprises and happy passions. Who could ask for more?

Believers in magic tell us that certain items, such as gems, as well as certain symbols, convey the meaning of love to those who know them. Wearing, holding or using such devices enhance your desirability, broaden your chances for amorous relationships and generally favor whichever aspect of lovemaking appeals to you, be it in the realm of dreams or in actions.

Here is a description of ancient amulets (things that are worn) and talismans (objects of magical power), all devoted to "amour."

In The Realm of Gems (From Indian Lore, 6th Century B.C.)

Diamond equals reconciliation in love and faithfulness.
Garnet equals loyalty and sincerity of heart.
Amethyst represents happiness and courage during adversity.
Sapphire causes repentance in face of faults.
Emerald equals hopeful love and knowledge of the future.
Ruby quiets excited passions and safeguards friendship.
Opal equals tenderness and faith.
Turquoise signifies successful love and marriage.
Topaz means eagerness in love and pleasant dreams.
Pearls represent purity, delicate feelings.

These jewels may be worn, of course, in rings. Golden rings enhance the ardent nature of each stone, while silver quiets passion, but stresses friendship and affection.

Love rings are usually in the design of intertwined chains, clasped hands or locked hearts. Cameos are well respected love amulets, as are pennies on a thin chain, necklaces with an odd number of pearls, chain-link bracelets, thin golden rings worn on the little finger (left hand) and tiny gold earrings which pierce the lobe.

The ancients ascribed certain colors to various degrees of love when worn or used in décor.

Bright red — strong passion
Red and black together — love turned to hatred
Dark red — violent passion
Light red or pink — affection
Yellow — sensuality
Green — cheerful love
Dark blue — over-bearing love
Light blue — purity, peace
Orange — blissful love
Brown — warmth

Those seeking the love of a reluctant individual should wear reds highlighted by yellow. Those desiring affection and chaste relationships should stick to blues and white — or pink if there is some minimal action desired. Newlyweds would do well to wear or live in warm browns and orange while older folk might let green be present in their lives, highlighted with touches of red (for a flavor of passion).

The color of the beloved's complexion must be noted here. "Distrust pale women," said Balzac, "but encourage those of a pink or orange hue." Among dark-skinned peoples, chestnut tones or bronze glows indicate passion and eager tenderness. Ruddy men are ardent lovers, as are black men with a purplish hue to their skin.

If one suffers from the aches of love — pain, whether real or imagined — resulting from unrequited passion, then pin a swatch of purple cloth close to your skin, say the old medicine men, and this will lessen the sorrow (but the problem will remain).

Specific symbols of love and sex are ever present in ancient veneration. In India the lingam (male) and the yoni (female) are often seen as amulets, as in the Egyptian Ankh, or life cross. Phallic stones and shapes were worshiped in Crete, in Greece, in India, as well as among early natives of North America. The Druids of northern France and the British Isles believed mistletoe to have erotic properties and wove it around their sacred oak trees. Thus today mistletoe at Christmas, and oak leaves throughout the year, are love symbols inviting a kiss if worn on the body or if held above the head.

A Potpourri of Love Talismans in Everyday Use

A shawl — marriage
A crystal glass — fidelity
A pair of gloves — a love affair
A vase — erotic love

Presents That Bespeak Magic Messages of Love

A plain golden ring — "I want you to marry me"
A chain — "Let us be bound together"
A pearl tie pin — "I seek your fidelity"
A walking stick — "Escort me through life"
A cameo — "You are the only one for me"
Gloves — "Let us have an affair"

Here Are Signals in the Form of Gifts Which Bode Ill

A belt — "You are domineering and cruel"
A hat pin — "You are an egotist"
A knife — "Let us break off"
A money purse or wallet — "You are too mercenary"

Lovers may draw signs or talismans to enhance their love or attract attention. Here is one derived from an old grimoire, a magic book of the medieval sorcerers.

On a parchment or cloth draw a circle about four inches in diameter within a circle. At the top of the outer circle pen in a simple cross. To the left of the cross draw a small circle with a dot inside (symbol of the sun). At the top of the cross, a star, and to the right, a half moon.

In the center of the circle write your beloved's name and within the border of the circle affix the double symbol of man and woman,

"Sun, Moon and Stars, by Venus and Mars..."

that is a circle with a cross attached to the bottom and an arrow attached to the top.

Now this talisman must be burned in the flame of a red candle at eleven p.m., while the supplicant yearns for his or her beloved and prays that the talisman be blessed by "Sun, Moon and Stars, by Venus and Mars . . ."

Zodiac signs in gold and bronze should be worn to enhance luck and love, but please make sure you wear the correct symbol, the one that is based on the *real stars* of the New Astrology not merely on the outdated signs.

Similar amulets include the Ankh of Egypt, the Hebrew Chai (for life)חי, a bit of ivory on a chain (meaning pure love), or a piece of coral (passion).

French ladies of the Empire period used to dip a finger in musk oil, or heavy perfume, and trace a "V" (for Venus) on their throat. This was intended to excite passion. A man may resort to a similar talismanic tactic; a bit of pipe tobacco squeezed between the fingers gives off an aroma "that women love" — according to popular lore — and a dash of patchouli on the neck will serve a multitude of similar ardent purposes.

4 The Magic of Nature

Ancient magicians, like Albert the Great of the thirteenth century, believed that wondrous magical powers reside in the realm of nature itself, in flowers, plants and other natural forms. Camphor, for instance, was reputed to reduce passion in men. Consequently, women of Napoleonic Europe were known to have sprinkled what we would call moth flakes in the pockets of their husbands' uniforms prior to long campaigns away from home.

Albert the Great recommends the burnt hairs of a wolf, sprinkled in wine, as a female "deflator." "When a woman drinks thereof," he wrote, "she shall desire no other man than her husband."

Also useful as a test of virtue, says Albert, is a certain stone called Magnes which could be found "in the sea of Inde." This stone should be placed at night under a woman's pillow, whereupon she will immediately embrace her husband or immediately "fall forth of her bed." In the later case the sorry husband will know he has been made a cuckold, at which time, according to rustic superstition, a pair of goat horns will sprout on his forehead.

Far more pleasant are the ancient notions of flower magic in regards to love.

It is said that the lovers of the Arabian Nights invented a language of flowers by discovering the magic meaning of each bloom then combined the appropriate flowers in a bouquet, or nosegay, so that the amorous message could be passed undetected to the well-guarded harem ladies.

Thus a cluster including forget-me-not, myrtle and heliotrope when "read" by the recipient spelled out the message: "Do not forget me while we are apart. I adore you."

From the lore of the Arabian nights we offer this "code" of love via the magic of flowers. By arranging nosegays, bouquets, and corsages appropriately you too can convey — without a single word — the most delicate, ardent or even petulant messages. (If that's not magic, what is?)

Arbutus — "Thee only do I love"
Beech — "Lover's tryst"
Bittersweet — "Truth"
Broken straw — "Quarrel"
Camellia — "Perfect loveliness"
Carnation — "Pure and deep love"
Cyclamen — "Diffidence"
Everlasting pea — "Wilt thou go with me?"
Flowering almond — "Hope"
Forget-me-not — "Do not forget me"
Four-leaved clover — "Be mine"
Garden daisy — "I share your feelings"
Goldenrod — "Encouragement"
Heliotrope — "I adore you"
Holly — "Am I forgotten?"
Hyacinth — "Constancy"
Ivy — "Marriage"
Jonquil — "Affection returned"

Lesser celandine — "Joys to come"
Lily of the valley — "Return of happiness"
Lupine — "Dejection"
Musk rose — "Capricious beauty"
Myrtle — "Love in absence"
Orange flower — "Chastity"
Peach blossom — "I am your captive"
Pennyroyal — "Flee away"
Peppermint — "Warmth of feeling"
Periwinkle — "Sweet memories"
Phlox — "Our hearts are united"
Pink larkspur — "Fickleness"
Plum blossom — "Keep your promises"
Quince — "Temptation"
Ranunculus — "You are radiant with charms"
Red rose — "I love you"
Sweet pea — "Meeting"
Sweet sultan — "Happiness"
Vervain — "Enchantment"
White clove — "I promise"
White straw — "Union"
Zinnia — "I mourn your absence"

With the above in mind, can you imagine what the following bouquet implies: flowering almond, red rose, four-leaved clover and ivy?

To this exquisite message those in love would likely reply with a sprig of arbutus. Would you?

There are besides flowers certain plants and herbs deemed magical in questions of love, none more strange or compelling than the fabled mandrake or mandragora.

Botanists call this plant *Mandragora officinarum* and warn that the juices of its roots and berries may be harmful, even deadly. Such knowledge did not inhibit the biblical Reuben, son of Jacob, in Genesis

30: 14-15, from digging up mandrakes as a present for his mother, Leah. Homer, for his part, tells us that the sorceress Circe used this plant to transform men into beasts.

The aphrodisiac reputation of mandrake no doubt derives from the shape of its roots, which often resemble a human form, the head being the leafy growth, the roots branching off into arms, trunk and legs. Because of this likeness, magicians of the twelfth and thirteenth centuries urged their lovesick followers to dig for these plants as love stimulants. The black variety should be sought by men, for this is allegedly the female mandrake; the white by women. The berries of either, when pressed, result in a narcotic brew; the roots when drained produce poison. However, in proper proportions these extracts

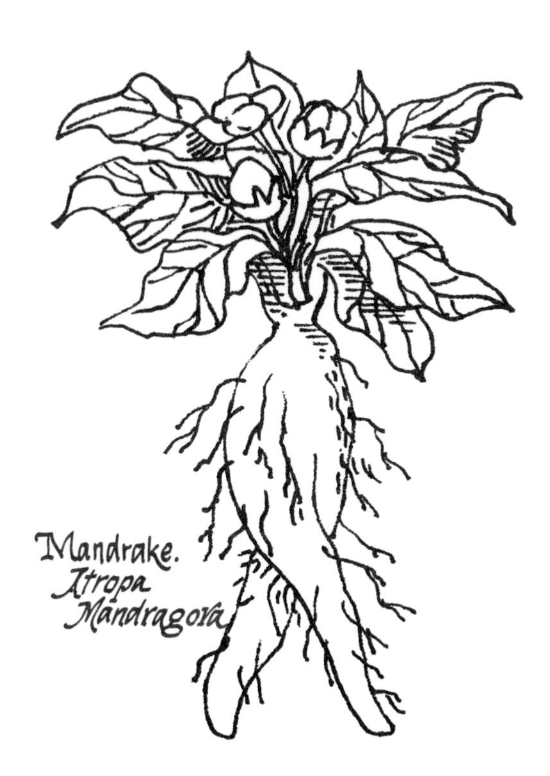

supposedly cause intense passion, magical power and erotic sleep.

Digging for the mandrake was no simple matter. The plant would yield only during a moonless night and only after hideous screeching and screams, screams which heard too closely would cause instant insanity or death.

To guard against such ends, the supplicant was urged to tie a long cord around the head of the mandrake, which appears above the ground. The other end of this cord is then tied around the neck of a dog who is enticed with food to jerk forward and thus extract the screaming plant. Being the actual digger, the dog thus dies and is buried in the mandrake's vacant hole.

Those who may not wish to tamper with the herb's potent juices (how wise they are), but who nevertheless seek the powers of mandrake, are advised to wear a piece of it on a cord around their necks. Because of its fetid odor, mandrake will repel all but one's own true love. He or she will yield gratefully to its intoxicating attraction.

Less exotic plants and foods of magical repute, in the realm of love, are such popular everyday items as lettuce, endive, laurel and carrots. Poppyseeds are also thought to inspire "amour." Ginger is considered a love stimulant as well. Gingerbread men (cookies shaped in human form) were favorites of Colonial American women, especially those in Salem, who had learned their recipes from Caribbean slaves.

Ginger was mixed with sweet batter, which was then rolled flat. Women in love, or disappointed wives, would proceed to cut male figures into the dough and then arrange the forms on a cookie sheet. The index finger was next pressed on the heart of each cookie and the batch was baked.

Eaten with tea, or another hot beverage, the cookie was supposed to inspire tender or ardent feelings in the male. Apparently it did and the pious New England men thought themselves bewitched. When the so-called witches of Salem were arrested, unbaked gingerbread cookies found in their houses were a part of the evidence used against them.

5 Love Potions & Perfumes

Intoxicating love philtres and perfumes, guaranteed to attract even the most adamant being, are concocted to stimulate everything from tender romance to flaming desire.

The notion of love philtres is one of the most delightful in literature and in opera. In the later category there are two potions of renown: the bubbling mixture of Dr. Dulcamara in Donizetti's *Elixir of Love* — a potion that is largely made up of good strong burgundy wine — and the mysterious, tragic Liebestrank, or love drink, of Wagner's *Tristan and Isolde*. The recipe for this transfixing brew is not provided by the composer, but we do have extant a few concoctions that the old grimoires presumed to be at least temporarily effective.

A German text recommends the following recipe: mix 20 grammes of essence of cloves, 10 grammes of essence of geranium with 200 grammes of alcohol; then heat at 90 degrees. Do not drink — but rather rub on the surface of the skin in a heated room. The effect, it is said, is aphrodisiac.

The Chinese advocate drinking warm ginseng tea, a delightful plum-like fruit, as a love stimulant of magical powers. The magician, Albert the Great, insists that dry periwinkle, powdered, and mixed with powdered earthworm induces love (or nausea). Less revolting is a philtre of thyme, majoram, fennel, wild mint and lily immersed in lustral (or spring) water.

Rain water is also supposed to induce romance falling from heaven as it does. One must drink it, of course, after it has been boiled. Gascon wine, heated with ginger, nutmeg and assorted savory spices is reputed by French savants to cause amorous attraction. And the American Indian had a "marriage" beer fermented of hops, to which crushed pine needles were added with the blessing of the moon goddess, Natoma.

From ancient Egypt to the modern day, perfumes have played a centrific role in romance. Sorcerers believed the appropriate combination of scents worn in conjunction with the correct color, and on the proper day, was bound to create an irresistible atmosphere of love. The formulas for two such perfumes are still extant.

Friday's scent (worn on Fridays, the day of Venus, in tandem with warm colors) is made from musk, ambergris, aloe wood and red rose petals — all reduced to a powder, mixed with the blood of doves, rolled into a paste and then consecrated with the words "Deus Abraham, bless all the creatures of the kinds contained in these fragrances so that their seductive powers may increase."

The paste is then applied behind the ears, on the breast and on the wrists.

Monday's perfume was less exotic in quality, intended to provoke affection, gentle interest and tenderness as befits the day of the moon.

It is compounded of the seed of white poppy, benzoin and camphor mixed with the blood of a turtledove and dedicated to Selene, goddess of the moon. It is most effective when worn with white, blue and gray.

Today the elegant essences of famous perfumes may perform similar services for the female in love, as will a strong scent like patchouli for the ardent male. Magicians say that the ardor of love enhances the scent and makes it irresistible, but that frigid feelings cause even the best, most powerful perfume to fade — or freeze — and lose its potency.

The early nineteenth-century sorcerer, Francis Barrett, author of *The Magus,* exhorted his followers to produce scented candles for occultic purposes, especially for the purpose of love.

Gold-colored candles, in which honey was blended with the wax, will cause sweet passion and clear sightedness. Red candles, stained with the blood of doves and scented with cinnamon — says Barrett — can evoke ardent desire. Whereas burning candles blended with wine causes a form of romantic intoxication.

Burning of incense in the boudoir or in the parlor — depending on one's circumstances and purposes — was advocated by many witches. Today one can purchase a wide variety of these scents manufactured in the Hindu style on jinn sticks. Delicate fragrances like vanilla, lemon, rose and violet will help arouse tenderness and compassion. Spicy odors (patchouli, black pepper, cinnamon) stimulate ardor and aggression.

Barrett believed grape incense causes men to fall at the feet of women as though drunk; whereas lemon, or lime, creates a more subdued and dignified atmosphere of courtship and romance.

Everyone has his or her favorite scent. Attempt to discover which it is your lover craves then use it accordingly before your rendezvous. Such devices, along with the correct lighting (such as candle light), the proper colors and refreshments (love philtres included) will — according to occultic cant — produce extraordinary results and magical memories.

Can you discover what kind of romances, which new faces, what emotions of love will soon befall you? The clairvoyants and seers of fifteenth-century France believed that certain oracles — signs of the future — or omens — everyday signs and symbols — could convey this very sort of information to those who know the secrets of discovery.

Among the most familiar of these was the Oracle of the Daisy. In this simple operation the one in love picks a daisy, (a white one is preferable) and proceeds to pluck each petal from the center, alternately saying: "He loves me — he loves me not." If the last petal to be plucked coincides with "He loves me" then, say the seers, you may rejoice, for your lover will soon declare himself. Less rejoicing will obviously accompany the negative reply.

Another version of the Daisy Oracle seeks to learn the intensity of love. As each petal is plucked, you ask "Does he love me a little" (pluck); "very much" (pluck); "passionately" (pluck); "madly" (pluck); "not at all" (pluck)? Whichever word coincides with the last petal, that is the one that conveys the truth.

Household items may serve as a lover's oracle, according to the French. Here is a popular selection from the elaborate Court of Versailles.

A needle if broken while you sew, indicates a young man who loves you from afar.

A match box upset may mean a wedding. If all the matches scatter, an early wedding. If any matches remain in the box, count each to see how many years will pass before the happy day.

Stockings put on unintentionally inside out mean a love present coming soon.

Should you break one blade of a pair of scissors this means a lovers' squabble in the offing. Should both snap off, then a break-up is predicted.

A lost garter means a proposal of love forthcoming; a garter found implies a love letter in the mail.

The sting of a bee — painful as it may seem — is a portent of passion; presence of ants refers to potential lovers' spats.

Broken eggs; beware of the sulks, the "blue devils."

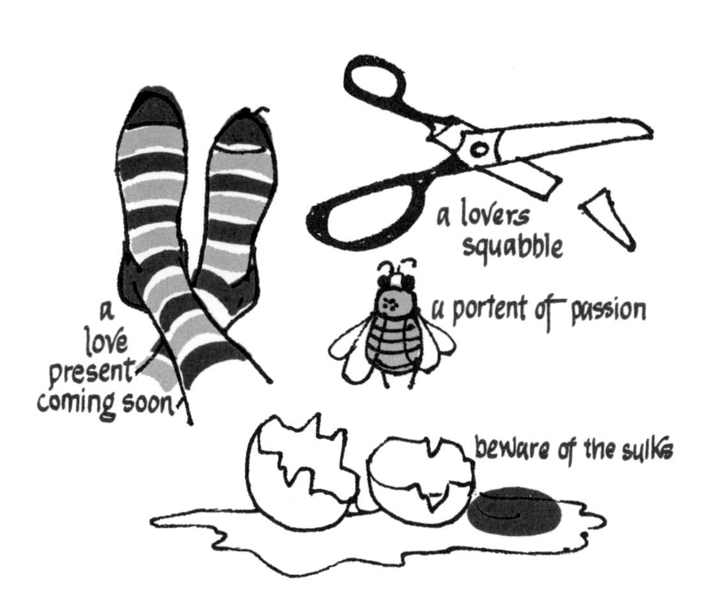

Wine glasses offer a whole compendium of oracles. Spilling over, or breaking, a wine glass filled with white wine is a good sign; if the wine is red it means anxiety; a rosé wine spilled implies hope. Should one tip over a full glass of wine or water this portends lasting love (despite the mess).

An Italian sage of the eighteenth century believed that physiognomy — the study of facial features — is a valuable "science" for those in love, since it reveals much hidden below the surface of the skin. It is thus a form of love magic, revealing that which is unknown. For example, the sage tells us, a young wrinkled forehead denotes a thoughtful mind; somewhat melancholy in love and likely to cause worry in the beloved.

If, in the face of a young woman, laughter brings a mass of lines at the corners of the eyes, then this is a good sign of moderation, but a pouting mouth implies a troublesome nature.

For perfection in love the following types are recommended (if one can ever find them). Women: finely shaped nose, strong mouth with fleshy lips, chin well marked but delicate, eyes full opened, eyebrows arched, ears close to the head and shell-like, and soft wavy hair. The male is similarly described: strong nose, high forehead, mouth not too wide but full, chin broad, hair soft and glistening.

Of course in addition to these obvious marks of physical perfection there are facial elements to beware, especially as concerns love. Small lazy eyes, for example, reflect an overly sensuous nature; deep-set eyes indicate a gloomy, wanton character; the proverbial hook nose refers to greed; while a pinched nose implies a straight-laced, priggish personality.

In the area of lips, slackness denotes a weak, wavering soul; tight lips may mean an insensitive person, who is not likely to admit his feelings. Chins are useful for determining the potential lover. A dimpled or cleft chin refers to discretion and sensitivity; a very sharp chin implies temper; a disappearing or receding chin may mean a shifty person; one likely to disappear himself.

As to hair; definitions of color — as outlined above — usually apply, to wit: bright red hair may mean a passionate, exhausting lover; bluish black hair, a deep energetic nature; soft brown tones imply sensitivity and gold or yellow symbolizes fairness, honor and nobility. Frizzy hair indicates a light-hearted nature; very curly hair: obstinacy; long silken tresses equals delicacy; short cropped hair — gaiety, and (this may surprise many) baldness in men: virility and ardor.

Albert the Great, the love seer of the Middle Ages, claimed that in order to know the depth of a woman's love it is necessary to measure the length of her left foot, divided in half. If the number is more than 4, her romantic potential is formidable. Others measure lips, forearms, and length of throat for the same information.

Quality of voice and laughter is also examined for love potentials. A honeyed voice means a sweet, sensitive love; a ribald, husky laugh surely implies a lusty nature; a silent laugh or giggle shows reserve; a laugh intermingled with sobs or gasps denotes a person of contrasting natures — and one who never laughs, or rarely does, gives strong indication that the individual is far from the happy realm of love and romance.

7 Games for Lovers

Throughout history, those in love have played their little games. Since we are dealing with The Magic of Love, we mean specifically games of chance and fortune intended to prophesy or indicate the course of romance and affection.

Four such games, which can be played by any couple in love, are presented here as examples. The tools for each are simple, the rules simpler still; the only challenge is to correctly assess the results and determine who may win — or lose.

The Forms of Fantasy (An Old Viennese Procedure)

In this bit of play, the lovers try to determine their fate by "reading" the message set forth by wax figures created spontaneously by each lover.

The following ingredients are needed: a large bowl filled with ice water, a hot plate or portable stove, a quantity of ordinary candle wax and a ladle.

The wax is melted and kept molten on the stove or hot plate. First the man dips the ladle into the wax then quickly dumps the hot wax into the ice-cold water. The wax will congeal at once. The resulting shape is then withdrawn and placed on a blotter or piece of paper towel. The lady proceeds to do the same.

When four shapes are laid out the "reading" can begin. The

following is a general guide to the waxen shapes that usually present themselves — magically or otherwise. Variations on each must be interpreted as one sees fit. It is important to relate the four shapes for a complete prophecy, adding other shapes if necessary.

Round, smooth shapes without projections indicate harmony, fulfillment, a fruitful relationship, smooth-going.

Jagged, peaked or craggy shapes mean difficult ways, thorny problems, excitement and adventure.

Obvious phallic shapes cannot be overlooked and, of course, imply the sexual and erotic aspects of love, as well as indications of possible short-lived relationships; those easily and quickly expended.

Elongated shapes, like pulled taffy, represent a long-lived relationship, endurance, good prospects and strength.

Pellets or broken shapes from one dip indicate offspring (for married couples), distractions, variety and fun.

Doughnut shapes — those with holes or spaces in them — portend ruptures, dissension, interlopers, and strain.

Humanoid shapes refer to other people interfering in your romance, either parents, rivals or society itself.

The possibilities are almost infinite, but the above should be a guide at least for a basic reading.

The Pendulum

Many have used Ouija boards for prophetic purposes. Here is a simplified version that can be made at home.

A piece of pumice, bought at any good drugstore, is carved in the shape of a pointer (or pear-shaped) and suspended by a ten-inch long piece of heavy duty thread.

Twelve cards of a regular poker deck are arranged in a circle. The deck is, of course, well shuffled in advance.

The lady goes first. She holds the pendulum, or pointer, by the thread at least three inches over the center of the circle, closes her eyes and lets the alleged magic forces of the universe take over. The pointer should swing toward one of the cards. For the meaning of that card, please refer to the section, *Divination of the Cards*.

For example, the pointer swinging to a Jack of Hearts indicates an attractive young lover soon to make himself known.

A simple "yes" or "no" question can be answered by the magic pendulum. An Ace of Spades is No, an Ace of Hearts, Yes. The two cards are placed three inches apart and the pendulum dangled over them. Again the forces governing love will move the pointer to one or the other. If, however, there is no motion, or the pendulum hovers between the two cards, the answer is neither yes nor no — but rather "maybe."

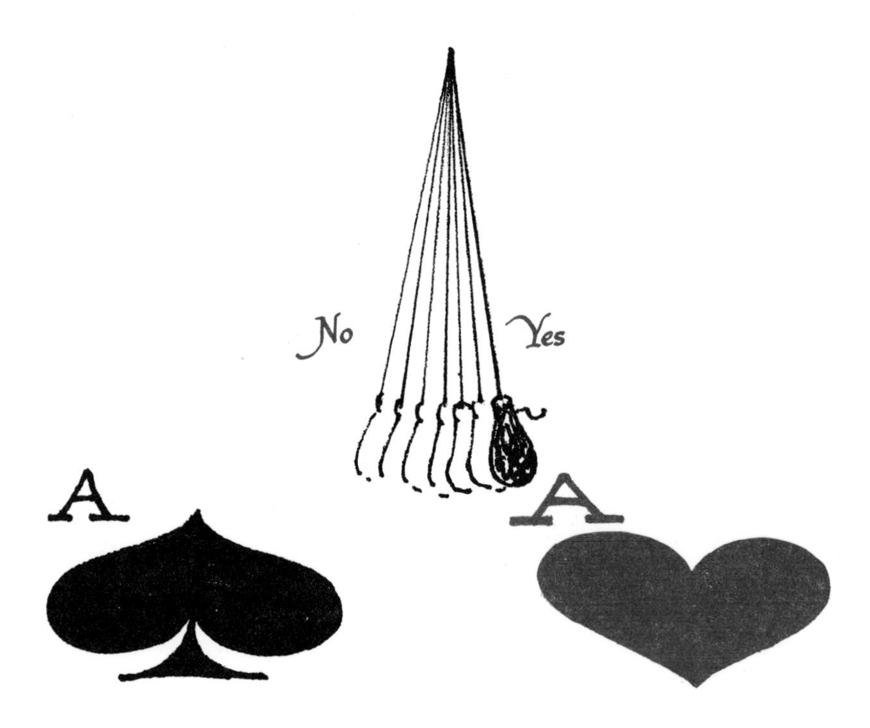

The Magic Ivories

The ivories involved are dice, ordinary game dice, tossed by those in love to answer specific questions. The magic involved has to do with numerology, the ancient divinational system of numbers.

Any combination may produce numbers from two to twelve (there is no chance of getting one unless only one die is used — which is not recommended by the seers). The code of numbers and answers is set forth below.

Two (snake-eyes) — doubtfulness, all things chancy, "maybe."

Three — positive; the implication of sexual success, good vibrations.

Four — No, not likely, never.

Five — a happy answer, a jolly one, implying fun and bright times.

Six — an indication of travel, a voyage, possibly a break-up.

Seven — strange doings, unsettled possibilities; the ending is unknown.

Eight — yes or no; up or down, good or bad; the number represents conflict.

Nine — high-minded love, reference to achievement, intellectualism.

Ten (like one) — strong, unified, the meaning of determination and progress.

Eleven — "Don't count on it."

Twelve — "Yes, yes, a thousand times yes."

One must be clever to properly assess the answers from this guide. For example, suppose the questioner — prior to tossing the dice — asks himself or herself, "Is this person the right one for me?" Clearly a four or a twelve indicates No or Yes respectively. But a three may mean Yes, but only in a physical way; or a nine, Yes but largely for intellectual friendship. A seven meanwhile would impart the sense of mystique and the unknown: give it a try, maybe you'll be surprised.

Random Pictures

Here is a game of chance for divinational purposes reportedly originated by psychic children in England with nothing to do on rainy afternoons.

One gets hold of a picture magazine, or a picture catalogue, and cuts out an array of basic pictures including faces, figures, buildings, cars, flowers, trees, landscapes — in short general items that are open to wide interpretations.

These are then pasted on index cards and thrown into a hat (or shoebox); one should use about twenty to twenty-five pictures.

The lovers each pick a picture at random keeping it out of sight. The man asks the girl a question pertaining to their romance, such as: "Do you love me only for my money?" She then reveals her picture, wherein the answer lies, according to the general guide listed below.

(Of course interpretation is the real "name of the game" and a clever individual need never be caught with the wrong answer.)

Here is the list of general interpretations of each random picture.

A young woman — positive sincerity, a meaningful reply.

A young man — yes, in a sensual, physical sense.

An old woman — a sign of interference, questioning, distraction.

An old man — symbol of authority, determination and strength.

A building or house — symbolizes honest intentions, domesticity and long-term planning.

A car or vehicle — indicates a tendency to waywardness also travel and motion.

A flower — tenderness and the sense of avowal.

A tree or landscape — peacefulness, complacency, contentment with simple things.

Children — the future, fruitfulness and happiness.

Animals — vigor, loyalty and strength.

Scenes of war or catastrophe indicate quite naturally strife and anxiety.

Miscellaneous: any picture may be interpreted on its face value or given a symbolic meaning. A horse, for example, can mean strength and swiftness or it can mean chance, as in a horse race.

To the original question about loving one for his money, the picture of an old man might imply: Not me, but my parents are so disposed; whereas a flower picture would clearly say: Never, not at all; mine is a tender feeling for you and has nothing to do with such mercenary thoughts.

The Beau Geste

Many are convinced that the body has a language of its own and that each gesture, sign, or movement can be interpreted in a quasi-magical way regarding various aspects of human fate.

In the area of love we may accept the old notion "every little movement has a meaning all its own" and therefore seek the secret messages lovers convey to each other by these means.

At the same time those in love can learn which gestures refer to what and thus practice this subtle form of love-making when in the company of their beloved — *or* with attractive strangers who may be "hip."

Gestures of Love for Ladies

Gently stroking the earlobe means "I want to be caressed."

Slowly running the tongue across the lower lip — "I crave your kisses."

Hands folded in the lap — "I seek a chaste relationship."

One hand stroking the throat — "Try to seduce me."

Tossing one's head so that the hair undulates — "Try to catch me."

One hand on the breast — "Swear you love me and I am yours."

Stroking the ankles — "I am suspicious, but willing to try."

Removing one shoe with the opposite foot — "I am available."

Turning a ring on one's finger in circles — "I seek marriage or a serious relationship."

In addition there are many more obvious gestures that everyone can guess.

A man must be limited to a few basic meaningful (and decorous) movements. Such as:

Stroking the sideburns — "Do I interest you?"

Straightening the tie — "You interest *me*."

Tapping the lower lip — "You excite me."

Stroking the chin — "I am strongly attracted."

Poking at the breast pocket — "May I sit next to you?"

Both hands on the knees — "I am a no-nonsense type."

Some lovers invent their own little gestures and, above all, pet names that have secret — therefore magical — powers. Nonsense names, for example, indicate happy affection. Variations on the given name, like Peggy or Johnny, indicate a parental type of love. Descriptive nicknames like "Tiny," "Curly" show physical attraction. Word names such as "Love," "Sweetie," "Doll" indicate an open, frank and well-founded relationship.

Those who choose to call each other by the given name, without variation, are cool, formal types. But this does not mean that they cannot be "tenderized." Try a nonsense name on one of them and see. A Christopher who is called "Topo" might suddenly melt with ga-ga affection.

8 The Magic of Marriage

To George Bernard Shaw "Marriage is popular because it combines the maximum of temptation with the maximum of opportunity." To those in love marriage is the natural culmination of tender feelings and romantic avowals. A kind of magic has developed around marriage no less intriguing than the magic of love.

In primitive tribes, the ritual was invested with awe and was deemed rigidly sacred. In our own culture there is a similar feeling, along with a wide panoply of customs, superstitions and functions that derive in part at least from ancient magical idealizations.

The bride, for example, has always been a figure of veneration. Many believe it good luck to unexpectedly catch a glimpse of a bride in all her regalia. The moon is sometimes called the Bride of Night and in the Jewish faith the Sabbath is compared to a radiant bride.

In Greece and Rome, a bride was protected by Venus and no one might look upon her between her dedication to the goddess and the ritual of consummation — or the sacrifice to Hymen — god of marriage. Since Hymen's symbol was a veil brides were obliged to wear veils to retain their anonymity before the wedding night.

In modern times the veil covers the bride's face until the vows are exchanged, whereupon the new husband lifts the barrier to place a kiss on his new wife's lips. Thus is the "consummation" symbolized. Another modern aspect of bridal anonymity concerns the best man. In former times he was the only stranger entitled to look upon the prospective bride. Today he acts as a go between — and possibly as a stand-in (as he is in tribal custom) lest the bridegroom bolt.

In a sense the bridal veil is a magical entity: when it is in place, the bride is a divine vestal of Venus, when removed, she rejoins mortal society to take her place as a work-a-day wife.

Because the ancients believed the household to be a battleground between beneficent and hostile deities, it was thought that the new wife should not set foot into her husband's house before the demons were propitiated. Yet nothing could better satisfy the household gods than to have a young bride toss beans or rice at the hearth. Clearly it became necessary to discover a way of getting the bride into the house without having her set foot therein. The solution remains today, she is simply carried over the threshold by her mate and thus "magically" avoids the hostile gods.

The use of rice as propitiation is largely an oriental conceit. Throwing rice at the newlyweds similarly derives from the ancient custom of bestowing rice and other grains upon the happy couple to insure their fertility and sustenance. In the past the newlyweds took care to save the gifts thus given; today they happily dash away as the rice is thrown.

The bride for her part does some throwing of her own, she tosses her bouquet to prospective brides, emulating the classic custom wherein the bride sprinkled flowers on the altar of Venus in thanks for her happiness. Because the bride was considered a magical figure, and in fact retains some of that quality even today, anything she does is deemed lucky and positive. Catching her bouquet therefore insures a forthcoming marriage for the skilled "outfielder."

Much is made of the bride's special costume and adornment. Everywhere in the world the bride is garlanded or crowned and her attire invariably includes flowers and colors of luck and purity: white

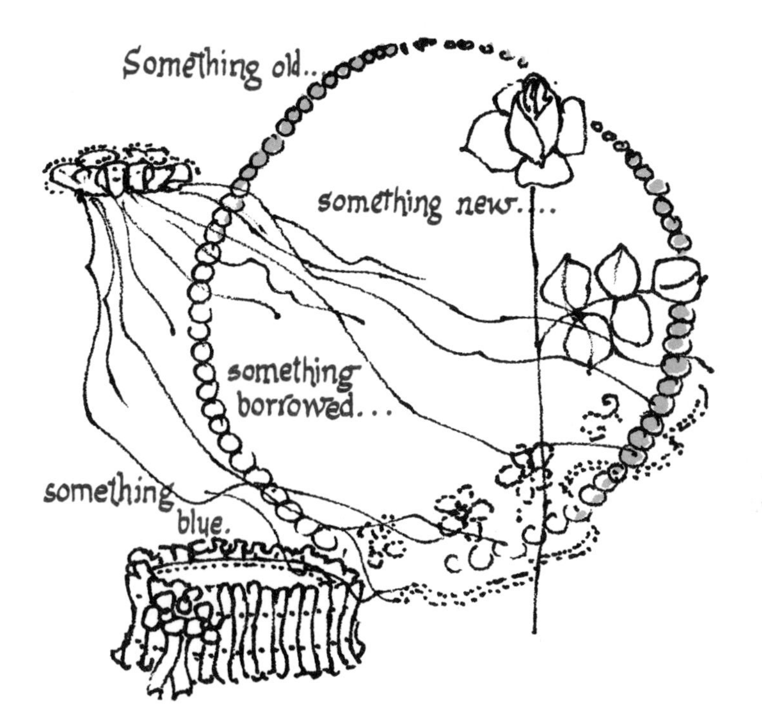

being the chief among these. Blue, which serves to remind us of modesty, heaven and serenity is also required in any bridal array. Amulets are no less useful especially of a love variety, such as a pearl necklace, a ring or garter. Frequently these are antiques used by a grandmother at her wedding. So far we have something old (the amulet), something blue — and as for that which is borrowed and new; borrowing insures the bride's return to her home so that she may return the borrowed item. In ancient times this was deemed appropriate because of the great distances often set up between the bride's family and that of her new husband. New items are universally endowed with positive force and luck, even as is the bride herself.

Some people tie old shoes to the newlyweds' car or carriage, a custom that derives from the idea that amidst the glamour and awe of the wedding there must be a homey touch to remind the couple of their forthcoming domestic responsibilities. In some cases each shoe represents a hoped-for child who will "follow" in his father's ways.

In some parts of the world noisemakers, such as tin cans, substitute for the shoes. And in the American West the "Shivaree" is performed as the couple takes to its bridal chamber. This raucous ceremony consists of much shouting, hazing, and merrymaking, all descended from the days when kinfolk felt it was necessary to shout away the hostile spirits from the newlyweds' door.

With marriage often comes turbulence, and the sorcerers of old looked for wedding omens that might denote ill luck or trouble. Should the wedding ring drop before it reaches the bride's finger, or should it slip, this implies divorce or an unhappy marriage they say. Should the bridal gown be stained by wine or mud, this too bodes ill. Or should any interloper break up the festivity, then there will be deception in the marriage. For that reason many wedding ceremonies include a call for "all those who may know of any reason why these two should not be joined in holy wedlock." If such a one does not come forth, the marriage will likely prosper.

Above all, the wedding ceremony itself implies happiness, fertility and love — as well as magic, beginning with the procession of bride and bridesmaids, which imitates the entrance of the vestal virgins into the temple of Vesta (Roman goddess of hearth and home), to the tossing of rice and flowers. Solemnity is often present at such times as when, in Jewish ceremonies, the bridegroom crushes a wine glass beneath his foot to recall the fall of Solomon's temple.

But in the long run the mirth and joy of the wedding and the feast that usually follows — another custom from ancient times — connotes the intended bliss every married couple envisions "for better or worse."

An Afterthought

To those in love, magic indeed seems to pervade the world, where each gesture, each thought becomes invested with wondrous qualities. But is this, in fact, *real* magic, the type sorcerers conceived, the sort enunciated in the previous pages? Or is it a kind of magic of the mind, a subtle psychological suggestibility that causes a simple necklace to become a powerful amulet or enables a certain color or flower to enhance love and luck?

Most sensible people will agree that magic is mostly within us; that elaborate rituals, involving incense, candles and ancient gods serve only to heighten our own emotions and thus give the semblance of cause and effect. Similarly, when a girl in love wears a bright red blouse, adorns herself in charms and splashes seductive perfume on her body, she somehow — subconsciously — becomes a modern-day Venus and a creature of magical love. But it is not the blouse or the scent itself that conveys romantic allurement, rather it is the new-found confidence and verve which these appurtenances intensify. That is what creates success (when it does) for the individual in question.

How precarious our lives would be if "magic" were to replace true love and sentiment and true integrity. How fallacious if "the supplicant" seeks only gratification via magic, and not a union of love. In these cases, as well, it is not the particular candle or potion that will do any good, but rather the eagerness or desperation of the individual, which will telegraph itself and be taken as a signal for exploitation or even abuse by insensitive people.

And so while it is true that "magic" has its own rules and that the aforementioned nostrums and novelties may indeed work their wonders whether by "true" sorcery or by more logical means, it is also true, as Dr. Johnson said, that "Love is the wisdom of the fool and the folly of the wise."

With this in mind we suggest proceeding with a rational approach to the magic recited herein, remembering that the magic of love is stronger than any sorcery.